Hugging Face Transformers for AI Automation

A Practical Guide to AI Automation, Model Fine-Tuning, and Scalable Deployment

Contents

Introduction

Chapter 1: Understanding Transformers

- Overview of Transformer Architecture
- How Transformers Differ from Traditional Neural Networks
- Applications of Transformers in AI Automation
- Why Hugging Face is the Industry Standard

Chapter 2: Setting Up Your Environment

- Installing Hugging Face Transformers
- Setting Up a Virtual Environment with Python
- Integrating PyTorch and TensorFlow
- Managing Dependencies Efficiently

Chapter 3: Exploring Pre-Trained Models

- What Are Pre-Trained Models?
- Hugging Face Model Hub: Key Resources
- Selecting the Right Model for Your Task
- Fine-Tuning vs. Transfer Learning

Chapter 4: Tokenization and Data Processing

- Understanding Tokenization in NLP
- Tokenizer Options: Byte-Pair Encoding, WordPiece, and SentencePiece
- Efficient Data Preprocessing Techniques
- Handling Custom Datasets with the Hugging Face Dataset Library

Chapter 5: Training and Fine-Tuning Models

- Steps to Fine-Tune a Pre-Trained Transformer
- Optimizing Hyperparameters
- Training on GPUs and TPUs
- Best Pract_xices for Large-Scale Training

Chapter 6: Deploying AI Models with Hugging Face

- Deploying Models via Hugging Face API
- Using Transformers in a Production Pipeline
- Integrating with Cloud Services (AWS, Google Cloud, Azure)
- Optimizing Performance and Scaling

Chapter 7: Automating AI Workflows with Hugging Face

- Leveraging Pipelines for Rapid Development
- Automating Model Selection and Fine-Tuning
- Using Hugging Face for Conversational AI and Chatbots
- Streamlining AI Pipelines with Hugging Face Accelerate

Chapter 8: Advanced Techniques

- Multi-Modal Transformers for Image, Text, and Audio Processing
- Training Custom Transformer Architectures
- Using Hugging Face Reinforcement Learning Models

- Integrating Hugging Face with AutoML for Automated Model Selection

Chapter 9: Best Practices and Troubleshooting

- Common Issues in Transformer Training
- Debugging Model Performance Problems
- Ensuring Ethical AI and Bias Mitigation
- Keeping Up with the Latest Hugging Face Updates

Conclusion

By mastering Hugging Face Transformers, professionals can unlock new possibilities in AI automation, streamline workflows, and build cutting-edge AI solutions efficiently.

Additional Resources

- Hugging Face Documentation
- Transformer Research Papers
- Online Courses and Tutorials
- Community Forums and GitHub Repositories

Hugging Face Transformers for AI Automation

A Practical Guide to AI Automation, Model Fine-Tuning, and Scalable Deployment

Introduction

Transformers have revolutionized the field of artificial intelligence, powering state-of-the-art models for natural language processing (NLP), computer vision, and beyond. From OpenAI's GPT models to Google's BERT, transformers now dominate AI applications, enabling unprecedented accuracy, efficiency, and scalability.

Among the many platforms that offer transformer-based models, **Hugging Face** has emerged as the go-to ecosystem for AI practitioners. With its powerful **Transformers** library, user-friendly APIs, and an extensive model hub, Hugging Face simplifies the process of deploying and fine-tuning transformers for real-world automation.

This guide is designed for AI automation professionals who want to **leverage Hugging Face Transformers effectively**. Whether you're a machine learning engineer, data scientist, or AI architect, this book will provide the essential knowledge and hands-on expertise you need to integrate Hugging Face models into your AI workflows.

Chapter 1: Understanding Transformers

Overview of Transformer Architecture

The transformer model, introduced in the paper *Attention Is All You Need* by Vaswani et al. (2017), revolutionized deep learning by replacing recurrent and convolutional architectures with a self-attention mechanism. The core components of transformers include:

- **Self-Attention Mechanism**: Unlike traditional sequential models, transformers process input in parallel by weighing the importance of different words in a sentence using attention scores.
- **Positional Encoding**: Since transformers lack recurrence, positional encoding allows them to retain word order information.
- **Multi-Head Attention**: By using multiple attention heads, transformers capture different types of contextual information.
- **Feed-Forward Networks**: Fully connected layers further refine the processed information.
- **Layer Normalization & Residual Connections**: These enhance training stability and model efficiency.

This architecture enables transformers to excel in various AI tasks, such as text generation, sentiment analysis, translation, and even image processing.

How Transformers Differ from Traditional Neural Networks

RNNs and LSTMs vs. Transformers

- **Parallelization**: Unlike recurrent models, transformers process entire sequences at once, drastically reducing training time.
- **Long-Term Dependencies**: Traditional RNNs struggle with remembering information over long sequences due to vanishing gradients, while transformers use attention mechanisms to maintain context efficiently.
- **Scalability**: Transformers can be scaled to massive datasets using architectures like BERT, GPT, and T5, whereas LSTMs face performance bottlenecks.

CNNs vs. Transformers

- **Feature Extraction**: While CNNs are effective at recognizing local patterns in images, transformers (such as Vision Transformers - ViTs) use self-attention to model global dependencies, leading to superior performance in many vision tasks.
- **Flexibility**: Transformers have been adapted to handle text, images, and multimodal data, whereas CNNs are predominantly used for vision tasks.

Applications of Transformers in AI Automation

Transformers have enabled AI automation across various industries:

1. **Natural Language Processing (NLP) Automation**
   - Chatbots and virtual assistants (e.g., GPT-based customer support bots)
   - Automated content generation (e.g., AI copywriting, summarization tools)
   - Sentiment analysis for customer feedback monitoring
2. **Computer Vision**
   - Image captioning and object recognition
   - AI-driven video analytics for security and surveillance
   - Automated medical image diagnosis
3. **Finance and Business Intelligence**
   - Fraud detection using transaction analysis
   - Automated report generation
   - AI-driven stock market predictions
4. **Healthcare and Life Sciences**
   - AI-powered diagnostics and personalized medicine
   - Drug discovery through NLP-based biomedical research analysis
   - Virtual health assistants and medical transcription automation
5. **Software Development and DevOps**
   - Code generation and bug detection (e.g., GitHub Copilot)
   - Automated API documentation and AI-driven code refactoring
   - AI-assisted data pipeline optimization

Transformers have transformed the AI landscape by enabling these high-impact automation applications, making them indispensable in modern AI-driven industries.

Why Hugging Face is the Industry Standard

Hugging Face has become the **de facto standard** for transformer-based AI development due to several key advantages:

1. **Pre-Trained Model Hub**
   - Access to thousands of **state-of-the-art pre-trained models** for tasks such as text classification, translation, and question answering.
   - Models from major research labs, including OpenAI, Google, and Meta, are hosted on Hugging Face.
2. **User-Friendly API & Open-Source Library**
   - The **Transformers** library provides an intuitive API to load and fine-tune models with just a few lines of code.
   - Supports multiple frameworks, including TensorFlow and PyTorch.
3. **Efficient Fine-Tuning & Customization**
   - Hugging Face makes it easy to **fine-tune pre-trained models** with domain-specific datasets.

- Features **Trainer APIs**, making training scalable and efficient.
4. **Community & Enterprise Support**
   - Hugging Face has a **large developer community** and offers enterprise solutions like Inference Endpoints for deploying models in production.
5. **Seamless Integration with AI Pipelines**
   - Compatible with major cloud platforms (AWS, Azure, Google Cloud).
   - Works with **ONNX and TensorRT** for optimized model inference.

By using Hugging Face, AI professionals can **accelerate AI development, reduce costs, and deploy cutting-edge models efficiently**, making it an essential tool for AI automation.

Chapter 2: Setting Up Your Environment

Before diving into hands-on implementation with Hugging Face Transformers, you need to **set up a proper development environment** that ensures smooth execution and scalability. This chapter will guide you through:

- Installing Hugging Face Transformers
- Setting up a virtual environment with Python
- Integrating PyTorch and TensorFlow
- Managing dependencies efficiently

By the end of this chapter, you'll have a fully functional **AI automation environment** optimized for building and deploying transformer-based models.

Installing Hugging Face Transformers

The **Transformers** library by Hugging Face provides a simple way to access pre-trained transformer models. You can install it in a few steps.

Step 1: Install Python (if not already installed)

Hugging Face Transformers requires Python **3.8 or later**. Check your Python version with:

```
python --version
```

If you need to install Python, download it from python.org or use a package manager like `apt`, `brew`, or `choco` based on your OS.

Step 2: Install the Transformers Library

The simplest way to install Hugging Face Transformers is via `pip`:

```
pip install transformers
```

To install it with additional dependencies for NLP tasks like tokenization, use:

```
pip install transformers[torch]  # For PyTorch
pip install transformers[tf-cpu]  # For
TensorFlow
```

To verify the installation, run:

```
import transformers
print(transformers.__version__)
```

Setting Up a Virtual Environment with Python

Using a **virtual environment** is a best practice to isolate dependencies and avoid conflicts between multiple projects.

Step 1: Create a Virtual Environment

Create a virtual environment named `huggingface_env` using **venv**:

```
python -m venv huggingface_env
```

For **Anaconda users**, create an environment with:

```
conda create --name huggingface_env python=3.10
```

Step 2: Activate the Virtual Environment

For Windows:

```
huggingface_env\Scripts\activate
```

For macOS/Linux:

```
source huggingface_env/bin/activate
```

Your terminal prompt should now show `(huggingface_env)`, indicating the environment is active.

Step 3: Install Essential Packages

Once the virtual environment is activated, install essential libraries:

```
pip install transformers datasets accelerate
```

- `datasets`: Provides access to large AI-ready datasets.
- `accelerate`: Optimizes model training for GPUs and distributed computing.

Integrating PyTorch and TensorFlow

Hugging Face Transformers supports **both PyTorch and TensorFlow**, allowing flexibility in model training and deployment.

Installing PyTorch

Install PyTorch with GPU support for **better performance** (if you have a compatible NVIDIA GPU).

To install the latest stable version, visit PyTorch's official website and follow the installation command for your system.

For example, to install PyTorch with CUDA support:

```
pip install torch torchvision torchaudio --index-
url https://download.pytorch.org/whl/cu118
```

For CPU-only installation:

```
pip install torch torchvision torchaudio
```

Installing TensorFlow

If you prefer TensorFlow, install it using:

```
pip install tensorflow
```

For GPU acceleration, install the TensorFlow version that supports your CUDA drivers:

```
pip install tensorflow-gpu
```

Verifying Installation

To check if PyTorch is installed correctly, run:

```
import torch
print(torch.__version__)
print(torch.cuda.is_available())  # Should return
True if GPU is enabled
```

To verify TensorFlow installation:

```
import tensorflow as tf
print(tf.__version__)
print(tf.config.list_physical_devices('GPU'))  #
Should list available GPUs
```

Managing Dependencies Efficiently

To maintain a clean and reproducible development environment, follow these best practices:

1. Using `requirements.txt`

Save your installed packages for easy reinstallation:

```
pip freeze > requirements.txt
```

To install dependencies on a new machine:

```
pip install -r requirements.txt
```

2. Using `pipenv` for Dependency Management

For better dependency control, use `pipenv`:

```
pip install pipenv
pipenv install transformers torch
pipenv shell  # Activate environment
```

3. Keeping Libraries Updated

Regularly update your libraries to access the latest features and security patches:

```
pip install --upgrade transformers torch
tensorflow
```

Conclusion

By completing this chapter, you've:

--> Installed **Hugging Face Transformers**
--> Set up a **virtual environment**
--> Integrated **PyTorch and TensorFlow**
--> Learned **best practices for dependency management**

Here's **Chapter 3: Exploring Pre-Trained Models** for your **SEO-optimized guidebook** on Hugging Face Transformers.

Chapter 3: Exploring Pre-Trained Models

Pre-trained models are at the core of modern AI automation, providing powerful, reusable deep learning architectures for **NLP, vision, and multimodal tasks**. Hugging Face's **Model Hub** offers thousands of pre-trained models that can be fine-tuned for specific applications.

In this chapter, we will cover:

- What pre-trained models are and how they work
- How to navigate the **Hugging Face Model Hub**
- Choosing the right model for your use case
- The difference between **fine-tuning** and **transfer learning**

By the end of this chapter, you'll know **how to leverage pre-trained transformers efficiently** for AI-driven automation.

What Are Pre-Trained Models?

A **pre-trained model** is a deep learning model that has been trained on a massive dataset before being made available for public use. Instead of training a model from scratch (which is computationally expensive), pre-trained models provide a **strong starting point** with learned representations.

Why Use Pre-Trained Models?

--> **Saves Time & Resources** – Training a model from scratch requires enormous datasets and computing power.
--> **Improves Accuracy** – Models trained on diverse datasets generalize better to new tasks.
--> **Reduces Data Needs** – You can fine-tune models on **smaller, domain-specific datasets**.
--> **Proven Performance** – State-of-the-art models like **BERT, GPT, T5, and LLaMA** already achieve top-tier results.

Types of Pre-Trained Models

Hugging Face provides pre-trained models for various AI tasks:

Task	Example Models	Use Cases
Text Classification	BERT, DistilBERT, RoBERTa	Sentiment Analysis, Spam Detection
Text Generation	GPT-2, GPT-3, LLaMA, T5	Chatbots, Content Generation
Named Entity Recognition (NER)	BERT-CRF, XLM-R	Medical Records, Legal Document Analysis
Machine Translation	MarianMT, mBART	Translating Text Across Languages

Text Summarization	T5, BART, Pegasus	Generating Summaries for Articles
Speech Recognition	Wav2Vec2, Whisper	Transcribing Audio to Text

Hugging Face's **Model Hub** makes it easy to find and implement these models.

Hugging Face Model Hub: Key Resources

The **Hugging Face Model Hub** is a repository of **over 100,000 pre-trained models** that you can use directly in your projects.

Explore the Model Hub: https://huggingface.co/models

How to Search for Models

1. **Use Filters**: Search by task, library (PyTorch/TensorFlow), and dataset.
2. **Sort by Popularity**: See the most downloaded and best-rated models.
3. **Check Benchmarks**: Some models provide accuracy comparisons and benchmarks.
4. **Explore Model Cards**: Each model has a **model card** with details on training data, parameters, and performance.

Loading a Model from the Hub

Hugging Face makes it easy to load pre-trained models in just **a few lines of code**:

Loading a Text Classification Model (BERT)

```
from transformers import
AutoModelForSequenceClassification, AutoTokenizer

model_name = "bert-base-uncased"
model =
AutoModelForSequenceClassification.from_pretraine
d(model_name)
tokenizer =
AutoTokenizer.from_pretrained(model_name)
```

Loading a Text Generation Model (GPT-2)

```
from transformers import AutoModelForCausalLM,
AutoTokenizer

model_name = "gpt2"
model =
AutoModelForCausalLM.from_pretrained(model_name)
tokenizer =
AutoTokenizer.from_pretrained(model_name)
```

This allows you to **quickly implement a state-of-the-art model** in your AI automation pipeline.

Selecting the Right Model for Your Task

Choosing the right model depends on several factors:

1. Task Type

- **NLP tasks** → BERT, GPT, T5
- **Computer Vision** → ViT, DINO
- **Speech Processing** → Wav2Vec2, Whisper

2. Performance vs. Efficiency

- **BERT, GPT-3** → Powerful but computationally expensive
- **DistilBERT, ALBERT** → Faster and lightweight versions

3. Multilingual Capabilities

- **XLM-R, mBART, MarianMT** for cross-lingual applications.

4. Licensing & Usage Restrictions

- Some models have **commercial restrictions** (e.g., OpenAI's GPT-4 is closed-source).
- Open-source alternatives like **LLaMA, Mistral, Falcon** provide strong performance.

Fine-Tuning vs. Transfer Learning

Once you've selected a pre-trained model, you can customize it for your specific application. The two most common approaches are:

1. Fine-Tuning (Recommended for Most Cases)

Fine-tuning involves **training a pre-trained model on a smaller, task-specific dataset**. This allows the model to specialize in a particular task **without forgetting its general knowledge**.

Example: Fine-tuning BERT for sentiment analysis on Twitter data.

```
from transformers import Trainer,
TrainingArguments

training_args =
TrainingArguments(output_dir="./results",
num_train_epochs=3)
trainer = Trainer(model=model,
args=training_args, train_dataset=train_dataset)

trainer.train()
```

Pros:
--> High accuracy
--> Task-specific learning

Cons:
X Requires labeled data
X More computationally expensive

2. Transfer Learning (For Quick Prototyping)

Transfer learning **freezes most of the model's layers** and only trains the final classification head. This is useful when you **don't have much labeled data**.

```
for param in model.base_model.parameters():
```

```
param.requires_grad = False
```

Pros:
--> Faster training
--> Requires less data

Cons:
X Less flexible than full fine-tuning

Conclusion

In this chapter, we explored:

--> What **pre-trained models** are and why they are powerful
--> How to use the **Hugging Face Model Hub** to find models
--> How to **select the right model** for your AI automation needs
--> The difference between **fine-tuning and transfer learning**

Chapter 4: Tokenization and Data Processing

Tokenization is a critical step in NLP pipelines, as it **converts raw text into numerical representations** that transformers can process. Choosing the right tokenization method impacts **model accuracy, efficiency, and training speed**.

In this chapter, we'll cover:

- What **tokenization** is and why it matters
- Different **tokenizer types** (Byte-Pair Encoding, WordPiece, SentencePiece)
- Efficient **data preprocessing techniques** for Hugging Face models
- How to **handle custom datasets** using the Hugging Face **Datasets Library**

By the end of this chapter, you'll have a deep understanding of how to **prepare data for training, fine-tuning, and inference** in an AI automation pipeline.

Understanding Tokenization in NLP

What is Tokenization?

Tokenization is the process of **splitting text into smaller units (tokens)** that a model can understand. Tokens can be **words, subwords, or even individual characters**, depending on the tokenizer used.

Why is Tokenization Important?

--> **Bridges Human & Machine Understanding** – Text must be converted into numerical representations before being fed into a transformer model.

--> **Handles Complex Linguistic Structures** – Some languages don't use spaces (e.g., Chinese, Japanese), requiring advanced tokenization.

--> **Improves Model Efficiency** – Reducing vocabulary size and limiting input length speeds up training.

--> **Enables Transfer Learning** – Pre-trained tokenizers ensure compatibility with existing models.

How Tokenization Works in Transformers

1. **Input Sentence:**
   "Hugging Face's Transformers are powerful!"
2. **Tokenizer Splits Text into Tokens:**
   ```
   ['Hugging', 'Face', ''s', 'Transformers',
   'are', 'powerful', '!']
   ```
3. **Tokens Converted to IDs (Numerical Form):**
   ```
   [1023, 875, 125, 5632, 34, 982, 2]
   ```

4. **Model Processes Token IDs & Produces Output.**

The type of tokenizer used affects how text is split into tokens. Let's explore different tokenization approaches.

Tokenizer Options: Byte-Pair Encoding, WordPiece, and SentencePiece

Transformers use **subword tokenization** to balance vocabulary size and model performance. The most common tokenization methods are:

1. Byte-Pair Encoding (BPE)

BPE is a subword tokenization algorithm that merges the **most frequent adjacent character pairs** iteratively.

 Example:
"lowering" → `['low', 'er', 'ing']`
"lowest" → `['low', 'est']`
Since "low" is a common subword, BPE keeps it as a unit.

Pros:
--> Handles out-of-vocabulary words

--> Reduces vocabulary size
--> Works well for European languages

Cons:
X Doesn't capture complex morphology
X May split meaningful words too much

--> **Used by:** GPT-2, RoBERTa

---

2. WordPiece Tokenization

WordPiece, used in **BERT and DistilBERT**, is similar to BPE but selects subwords based on **likelihood rather than frequency**.

 Example:
"unhappiness" → `['un', '##happiness']`
"happiness" → `['happiness']`

--> Keeps frequent words intact
--> Works well for morphologically rich languages

X Can generate too many subwords for rare words

--> **Used by:** BERT, DistilBERT, ALBERT

---

3. SentencePiece Tokenization

SentencePiece doesn't require spaces and **treats text as a stream of characters**, making it effective for **multilingual tokenization**.

 Example:
"I'm learning NLP!" → `['_I', '''', 'm',`
`'_learning', '_N', 'L', 'P', '!']`

--> Works for languages without spaces (e.g., Chinese, Japanese)
--> Handles multilingual text efficiently

X Slightly more complex implementation

--> **Used by:** T5, mBART, MarianMT

Efficient Data Preprocessing Techniques

Before training a model, text data **must be cleaned and tokenized efficiently**. Here are key preprocessing techniques:

1. Cleaning Raw Text Data

Raw text may contain **HTML tags, special characters, and irrelevant symbols** that can reduce model accuracy.

Example Cleaning Code (Python)

```python
python

import re

def clean_text(text):
    text = text.lower()  # Convert to lowercase
    text = re.sub(r'\s+', ' ', text)  # Remove
extra spaces
    text = re.sub(r'[^\w\s]', '', text)  # Remove
special characters
    return text

sample_text = "Hello, World! NLP is amazing. <br>
Visit huggingface.co"
cleaned_text = clean_text(sample_text)
print(cleaned_text)
```

Output: "hello world nlp is amazing visit huggingfaceco"

---

2. Tokenizing Text Using Hugging Face Tokenizers

Hugging Face provides **AutoTokenizer**, which loads the right tokenizer based on the model.

Example: Tokenizing with BERT's WordPiece Tokenizer

```python
python

from transformers import AutoTokenizer
```

```
tokenizer = AutoTokenizer.from_pretrained("bert-
base-uncased")

text = "Hugging Face's Transformers are
powerful!"
tokens = tokenizer.tokenize(text)
token_ids =
tokenizer.convert_tokens_to_ids(tokens)

print("Tokens:", tokens)
print("Token IDs:", token_ids)
```

Output:

bash

```
Tokens: ['hugging', 'face', ''', 's',
'transformers', 'are', 'powerful', '!']
Token IDs: [7592, 2227, 1521, 1055, 19081, 2024,
3928, 999]
```

Handling Custom Datasets with the Hugging Face Datasets Library

Hugging Face provides the **Datasets Library** to load, preprocess, and manage large-scale NLP datasets.

1. Installing and Importing the Library

bash

```
pip install datasets
python

from datasets import load_dataset
```

```
dataset = load_dataset("imdb")  # Loads IMDb
movie review dataset
print(dataset["train"][0])  # Displays the first
training sample
```

--> **Supports CSV, JSON, and Parquet** formats

--> **Streaming mode** for large datasets

--> **Built-in NLP datasets (IMDB, SQuAD, Common Crawl, etc.)**

---

2. Custom Dataset Processing

To preprocess a **custom CSV dataset**, follow these steps:

```python
from datasets import load_dataset

# Load custom dataset
dataset = load_dataset("csv",
data_files="my_data.csv")

# Tokenize dataset
def tokenize_function(examples):
    return tokenizer(examples["text"],
padding="max_length", truncation=True)

tokenized_datasets =
dataset.map(tokenize_function, batched=True)
```

Conclusion

In this chapter, we covered:

--> **Tokenization methods** (BPE, WordPiece, SentencePiece)
--> **How tokenization affects NLP model performance**
--> **Efficient text preprocessing techniques**
--> **Handling large NLP datasets with Hugging Face Datasets**

Chapter 5: Training and Fine-Tuning Models

Fine-tuning **pre-trained transformer models** is a powerful way to customize AI for specific tasks. Whether you're working on **text classification, sentiment analysis, question answering, or translation**, fine-tuning lets you **leverage state-of-the-art models** without training from scratch.

In this chapter, we'll cover:

- **How to fine-tune a pre-trained transformer model**
- **Optimizing hyperparameters for better performance**
- **Training efficiently on GPUs and TPUs**
- **Best practices for large-scale training**

By the end of this chapter, you'll be able to **fine-tune Hugging Face models efficiently** for real-world applications.

Steps to Fine-Tune a Pre-Trained Transformer

Fine-tuning involves **taking a general-purpose pre-trained model** (like BERT, GPT, or T5) and adapting it to a **specific NLP task** with labeled data.

1. Choose a Pre-Trained Model

Hugging Face's **Model Hub** provides thousands of pre-trained models. You can browse available models here.

For example, if you want to fine-tune a **BERT model for text classification**, you can use:

```python
from transformers import
AutoModelForSequenceClassification
model =
AutoModelForSequenceClassification.from_pretrained("bert-base-uncased", num_labels=2)
```

`num_labels=2` is used for **binary classification** (e.g., sentiment analysis).

---

2. Load and Tokenize Your Dataset

Use the **Hugging Face Datasets library** to load and preprocess text data.

```python
from datasets import load_dataset
from transformers import AutoTokenizer

dataset = load_dataset("imdb")   # Load the IMDb
movie reviews dataset
tokenizer = AutoTokenizer.from_pretrained("bert-
base-uncased")

def tokenize_function(examples):
    return tokenizer(examples["text"],
padding="max_length", truncation=True)

tokenized_datasets =
dataset.map(tokenize_function, batched=True)
```

Truncation ensures text fits within the model's maximum token length.
Padding maintains uniform input size for batch processing.

---

3. Define a DataLoader

Hugging Face models require **PyTorch or TensorFlow DataLoaders** for efficient training.

```python
from torch.utils.data import DataLoader
from transformers import DataCollatorWithPadding

data_collator =
DataCollatorWithPadding(tokenizer=tokenizer)
```

```
train_dataloader =
DataLoader(tokenized_datasets["train"],
shuffle=True, batch_size=8,
collate_fn=data_collator)
```

Batch size affects memory usage and model performance.

---

4. Set Up Training Arguments

The **Trainer API** simplifies fine-tuning with automatic logging, evaluation, and checkpointing.

python

```
from transformers import TrainingArguments,
Trainer

training_args = TrainingArguments(
    output_dir="./results",
    evaluation_strategy="epoch",
    save_strategy="epoch",
    per_device_train_batch_size=8,
    per_device_eval_batch_size=8,
    num_train_epochs=3,
    logging_dir="./logs",
    logging_steps=100,
)

trainer = Trainer(
    model=model,
    args=training_args,
    train_dataset=tokenized_datasets["train"],
    eval_dataset=tokenized_datasets["test"],
    tokenizer=tokenizer,
    data_collator=data_collator,
```

)

`num_train_epochs=3`: Number of full passes over the dataset.
`evaluation_strategy="epoch"`: Evaluates the model at the end of each epoch.
`logging_steps=100`: Logs performance metrics every 100 steps.

---

5. Start Training the Model

Finally, train the model using:

```python
python

trainer.train()
```

`-->` The model **fine-tunes on the dataset** while tracking performance.

Optimizing Hyperparameters

Hyperparameter tuning improves model **accuracy, speed, and efficiency**.

1. Learning Rate Scheduling

The **learning rate (LR)** controls how much the model updates weights.

Too high → Model won't converge
Too low → Training is too slow

 Recommended values:

- **Fine-tuning transformers:** 2e-5 to 5e-5
- **Larger datasets:** 1e-4

--> Set the learning rate using the `TrainingArguments` parameter:

```python
training_args =
TrainingArguments(learning_rate=5e-5, ...)
```

---

2. Batch Size and Gradient Accumulation

Batch size affects **GPU memory and model stability**.
 Recommended batch sizes:

- Small GPU (8GB) → 8
- Large GPU (24GB+) → 32

If **GPU memory is limited**, use **gradient accumulation** to simulate a larger batch size:

```python
training_args =
TrainingArguments(gradient_accumulation_steps=4,
...)
```

--> This **accumulates gradients** before updating weights, reducing memory usage.

---

3. Weight Decay for Regularization

To **prevent overfitting**, add **weight decay**:

```python
python
```

```python
training_args =
TrainingArguments(weight_decay=0.01, ...)
```

--> **Weight decay** keeps model weights small, improving generalization.

Training on GPUs and TPUs

Transformers require **accelerated hardware** (GPUs or TPUs) for efficient training.

1. Training on a GPU (CUDA)

To train on a **GPU**, install PyTorch with CUDA support:

```bash
bash
```

```bash
pip install torch torchvision torchaudio --index-
url https://download.pytorch.org/whl/cu118
```

Check if GPU is available:

```python
import torch
print(torch.cuda.is_available())   # True if GPU
is detected
```

--> Train faster by using `fp16` mixed precision training:

```python
training_args = TrainingArguments(fp16=True, ...)
```

Benefit: Reduces memory usage and speeds up training.

---

2. Training on a TPU (Google Cloud/Colab)

For large-scale models, use **Google TPUs** with TensorFlow or PyTorch.
Enable TPU training by setting:

```python
training_args =
TrainingArguments(tpu_num_cores=8, ...)
```

--> TPUs offer extreme parallelism for massive datasets.

Best Practices for Large-Scale Training

Fine-tuning large models requires careful resource management.

--> Use Distributed Training

For multi-GPU setups, enable **Distributed Data Parallel (DDP):**

```python
training_args = TrainingArguments(
    per_device_train_batch_size=16,
    gradient_accumulation_steps=2,
    ddp_find_unused_parameters=False,
)
```

--> Use Model Checkpointing

Save model checkpoints to avoid losing progress:

```python
training_args = TrainingArguments(save_steps=500,
...)
```

--> Monitor Training with WandB or TensorBoard

To track metrics visually:

```bash
pip install wandb
wandb login
```

Modify training args:

```python
```

```
training_args =
TrainingArguments(report_to="wandb", ...)
```

Visualize accuracy, loss, and training curves in real time!

Conclusion

In this chapter, we covered:

--> **Fine-tuning pre-trained transformers**
--> **Optimizing hyperparameters for better accuracy**
--> **Training efficiently on GPUs and TPUs**
--> **Best practices for large-scale training**

Chapter 6: Deploying AI Models with Hugging Face

After training and fine-tuning your transformer model, the next step is **deployment**. Deployment ensures your model can be used **in real-world applications**, whether for **chatbots, text classification, or automated summarization**.

In this chapter, we'll cover:

- **Deploying models via Hugging Face API**
- **Using transformers in a production pipeline**
- **Integrating with cloud services like AWS, Google Cloud, and Azure**
- **Optimizing performance and scaling for high-demand applications**

By the end of this chapter, you'll be able to **deploy your AI model efficiently** and serve it to users.

Deploying Models via Hugging Face API

The **Hugging Face Inference API** is the easiest way to deploy a model **without managing servers**.

1. Upload Your Model to Hugging Face Hub

To deploy via the **Hugging Face API**, you need to first upload your fine-tuned model to the **Model Hub**.

Step 1: Install the Hugging Face CLI

bash

```
pip install huggingface_hub
```

Step 2: Log in to Hugging Face

bash

```
huggingface-cli login
```

You'll need an **API token**, which you can get from your Hugging Face account.

Step 3: Upload Your Model

python

```
from huggingface_hub import notebook_login

notebook_login()  # Logs in via your browser

model.push_to_hub("your-username/your-model-name")
tokenizer.push_to_hub("your-username/your-model-name")
```

Your model is now hosted on Hugging Face Hub and can be accessed via API!

2. Using the Inference API

Once uploaded, you can make API requests to **run predictions**.

Example: Text Classification API Call

```python
python

import requests

API_URL = "https://api-
inference.huggingface.co/models/your-
username/your-model-name"
headers = {"Authorization": f"Bearer
YOUR_HF_TOKEN"}

def query(payload):
    response = requests.post(API_URL,
headers=headers, json=payload)
    return response.json()

output = query({"inputs": "The product is
amazing!"})
print(output)
```

--> **No need to manage GPUs or infrastructure—**
Hugging Face handles everything!

Using Transformers in a Production Pipeline

If you need **custom API endpoints**, **real-time inference**,
or integration with other services, deploy the model using
FastAPI or Flask.

1. Create a FastAPI Endpoint

FastAPI is a **high-performance API framework** for serving models.

```python
python

from fastapi import FastAPI
from transformers import pipeline

app = FastAPI()
classifier = pipeline("sentiment-analysis",
model="your-username/your-model-name")

@app.post("/predict/")
def predict(text: str):
    return classifier(text)
```

Run the API with:

```bash
bash

uvicorn app:app --host 0.0.0.0 --port 8000
```

--> Now, your model is **accessible as an API** at
`http://localhost:8000/predict/`.

Integrating with Cloud Services (AWS, Google Cloud, Azure)

For **scalability and production-grade deployments**, host your model on a **cloud platform**.

1. Deploying on AWS Lambda (Serverless Inference)

AWS Lambda is a **cost-efficient, serverless** solution for inference.

Steps:

- Convert the model to `TorchScript` for **faster execution**.
- Package the model with a Lambda function.
- Deploy using **AWS API Gateway** for public access.

Convert Model to TorchScript:

```python
import torch

dummy_input = torch.randn(1, 512)   # Adjust based
on your model input size
traced_model = torch.jit.trace(model,
dummy_input)
traced_model.save("model.pt")
```

Upload `model.pt` to AWS Lambda and create a function for inference.

---

2. Deploying on Google Cloud AI Platform

Google Cloud AI allows you to **deploy and scale models easily**.

Steps:

- Convert the model to **TensorFlow SavedModel format** (if using TensorFlow).
- Upload to **Google Cloud Storage**.
- Deploy using **Vertex AI** for real-time serving.

Convert Model to TensorFlow Format:

```python
from transformers import TFAutoModel

tf_model = TFAutoModel.from_pretrained("your-
username/your-model-name")
tf_model.save_pretrained("saved_model")
```

--> Deploy using **Google Cloud Vertex AI** for auto-scaling inference.

---

3. Deploying on Azure Machine Learning

Azure ML supports **containerized model deployment** using **Azure Container Instances (ACI)**.

Steps:

- Package the model inside a **Docker container**.
- Deploy the container to **Azure ML Inference Server**.

Create a Dockerfile for Model Deployment:

```dockerfile
dockerfile

FROM python:3.9

RUN pip install transformers torch fastapi
uvicorn

COPY model /app/model
WORKDIR /app
CMD ["uvicorn", "app:app", "--host", "0.0.0.0",
"--port", "80"]
```

--> Push to **Azure Container Registry (ACR)** and deploy using **Azure Kubernetes Service (AKS)**.

Optimizing Performance and Scaling

For **high-demand applications**, optimize your deployment for **speed and scalability**.

1. Convert to ONNX for Faster Inference

ONNX (Open Neural Network Exchange) **reduces latency** by optimizing model execution.

Convert Model to ONNX:

```python
python

import torch
from transformers import AutoModel
```

```
model = AutoModel.from_pretrained("your-
username/your-model-name")
dummy_input = torch.randn(1, 512)
torch.onnx.export(model, dummy_input,
"model.onnx")
```

--> **ONNX models run up to 10x faster** than standard PyTorch models.

---

2. Use Model Quantization to Reduce Size

Quantization **reduces model size** while maintaining accuracy.

Apply 8-bit quantization:

```
python

from transformers import AutoModel

model = AutoModel.from_pretrained("your-
username/your-model-name")
quantized_model =
torch.quantization.quantize_dynamic(model,
{torch.nn.Linear}, dtype=torch.qint8)
torch.save(quantized_model.state_dict(),
"quantized_model.pth")
```

--> **Speeds up inference by up to 50%** with minimal accuracy loss.

---

3. Deploy with Kubernetes for Scalability

For handling **millions of requests**, use **Kubernetes (K8s)**.

- Deploy model containers on **Kubernetes cluster**
- Use **Horizontal Pod Autoscaler (HPA)** for scaling
- Optimize with **GPU-accelerated nodes**

Deploying in Kubernetes:

yaml

```
apiVersion: apps/v1
kind: Deployment
metadata:
  name: transformer-api
spec:
  replicas: 3
  template:
    spec:
      containers:
      - name: model-api
        image: your-docker-image
        ports:
        - containerPort: 80
```

--> **Kubernetes ensures automatic scaling and high availability.**

Conclusion

In this chapter, we covered:

--> Deploying models via Hugging Face API
--> Using transformers in a production pipeline
--> Integrating with AWS, Google Cloud, and Azure
--> Optimizing performance with ONNX, quantization, and Kubernetes

Chapter 7: Automating AI Workflows with Hugging Face

Building and deploying AI models can be **time-consuming** without automation. **Hugging Face** offers tools to simplify and speed up AI development through:

- **Pre-built pipelines for rapid prototyping**
- **Automated model selection and fine-tuning**
- **Conversational AI and chatbot integration**
- **Scaling AI workflows with Hugging Face Accelerate**

By the end of this chapter, you'll be able to **automate repetitive AI tasks, speed up model deployment, and build scalable workflows**.

Leveraging Pipelines for Rapid Development

What Are Hugging Face Pipelines?

Pipelines provide **pre-configured, easy-to-use** functions for common NLP tasks like:

--> **Text classification** (sentiment analysis, topic detection)
--> **Named entity recognition (NER)** (detecting people, locations, organizations)
--> **Text generation** (GPT-based models)

--> **Translation** (language conversion)

--> **Summarization** (compressing long texts)

Instead of manually loading models and tokenizers, **pipelines handle everything** for you!

How to Use Pipelines in Python

1. Install Hugging Face Transformers

```bash
pip install transformers
```

2. Load a Pre-Trained Pipeline

```python
from transformers import pipeline

# Load a sentiment analysis pipeline
classifier = pipeline("sentiment-analysis")

# Run inference
result = classifier("I love using Hugging Face!")
print(result)
```

Output:

```json
[{'label': 'POSITIVE', 'score': 0.9998}]
```

--> **No need for manual preprocessing or complex setup!**

Automating Model Selection and Fine-Tuning

1. AutoModel for Dynamic Model Loading

Instead of specifying a model manually, use **AutoModel** to dynamically select the best available model.

Example: Load the Best Text Classification Model Automatically

```python
from transformers import
AutoModelForSequenceClassification, AutoTokenizer

model_name = "distilbert-base-uncased-finetuned-
sst-2-english"
tokenizer =
AutoTokenizer.from_pretrained(model_name)
model =
AutoModelForSequenceClassification.from_pretraine
d(model_name)
```

--> **This approach ensures compatibility across different models without hardcoding them.**

---

2. Automate Fine-Tuning with Trainer API

Fine-tuning is **resource-intensive**, but the **Trainer API** simplifies it by:

--> Handling **dataset loading & tokenization**
--> Automating **hyperparameter tuning**
--> Optimizing with **GPU acceleration**

Example: Fine-Tuning a Model Automatically

```python
from transformers import Trainer,
TrainingArguments

training_args = TrainingArguments(
    output_dir="./results",
    evaluation_strategy="epoch",
    save_strategy="epoch",
    per_device_train_batch_size=8,
    per_device_eval_batch_size=8,
    num_train_epochs=3,
    logging_dir="./logs",
)

trainer = Trainer(
    model=model,
    args=training_args,
    train_dataset=train_data,
    eval_dataset=eval_data,
)

trainer.train()
```

--> Automates the entire fine-tuning process with minimal setup!

Using Hugging Face for Conversational AI and Chatbots

Building a Chatbot with a Pre-Trained Transformer

Hugging Face provides **state-of-the-art chatbot models** like:

- **DialoGPT** (OpenAI's GPT-based conversational AI)
- **BlenderBot** (Facebook AI's advanced chatbot)

1. Install the Required Libraries

bash

```
pip install transformers
```

2. Load a Pre-Trained Chatbot Model

python

```
from transformers import pipeline

chatbot = pipeline("conversational",
model="microsoft/DialoGPT-medium")

response = chatbot("What is your favorite
movie?")
```

```
print(response)
```

--> No need to build a chatbot from scratch—just fine-tune an existing one!

---

3. Deploying a Chatbot as a Web App

To make your chatbot **accessible online**, use **FastAPI**.

Example: Building a FastAPI Chatbot Endpoint

```python
python

from fastapi import FastAPI
from transformers import pipeline

app = FastAPI()
chatbot = pipeline("conversational",
model="microsoft/DialoGPT-medium")

@app.post("/chat")
def chat(input_text: str):
    return chatbot(input_text)
```

--> Now your chatbot is accessible via an API at `http://localhost:8000/chat`!

Streamlining AI Pipelines with Hugging Face Accelerate

What Is Hugging Face Accelerate?

Hugging Face Accelerate is a **framework for distributed training**, enabling:

--> **Multi-GPU and TPU training**
--> **Automatic batch size scaling**
--> **Seamless model parallelism**

---

1. Install Hugging Face Accelerate

bash

```
pip install accelerate
```

2. Configure Accelerate for Multi-GPU Training

bash

```
accelerate config
```

You'll be prompted to **select the number of GPUs** and **memory settings**.

---

3. Convert a PyTorch Model to Accelerate for Faster Training

python

```
from accelerate import Accelerator
```

```
accelerator = Accelerator()
model, optimizer, train_dataloader =
accelerator.prepare(model, optimizer,
train_dataloader)

for batch in train_dataloader:
    with accelerator.accumulate(model):
        outputs = model(**batch)
        loss = outputs.loss
        accelerator.backward(loss)
        optimizer.step()
```

--> Speeds up training without modifying your existing model code!

Conclusion

In this chapter, we explored:

--> Pipelines for quick AI development
--> Automated model selection & fine-tuning
--> Building chatbots using Hugging Face models
--> Scaling AI workflows with Hugging Face Accelerate

Chapter 8: Advanced Techniques

As AI evolves, **transformers are no longer limited to NLP**. Advanced techniques allow you to:

- **Process text, images, and audio with multi-modal transformers**
- **Train custom transformer architectures** for specialized tasks
- **Use reinforcement learning (RL) for AI agents**
- **Automate model selection with AutoML**

By the end of this chapter, you'll master **cutting-edge transformer applications** and **enhance AI automation workflows**.

Multi-Modal Transformers for Image, Text, and Audio Processing

What Are Multi-Modal Transformers?

Multi-modal transformers **combine different data types** (text, images, audio) into a single model.

Popular examples include:

- **CLIP (OpenAI)** → Understands text-image relationships
- **DALL·E** → Generates images from text prompts
- **Whisper** → Converts speech to text

- **BLIP-2** → Vision-language model for advanced AI tasks

---

1. Using CLIP for Image-Text Processing

CLIP can **match text descriptions to images** or **classify images** based on textual input.

Example: Classify an Image with CLIP

python

```
from transformers import CLIPProcessor, CLIPModel
from PIL import Image
import requests

# Load pre-trained CLIP model
model = CLIPModel.from_pretrained("openai/clip-
vit-base-patch32")
processor =
CLIPProcessor.from_pretrained("openai/clip-vit-
base-patch32")

# Load an image
url =
"https://huggingface.co/datasets/huggingface/docu
mentation-
images/resolve/main/transformers/tasks/CLIP_examp
le.jpg"
image = Image.open(requests.get(url,
stream=True).raw)

# Define labels
labels = ["a dog", "a cat", "a person", "a car"]
```

```python
# Process input
inputs = processor(text=labels, images=image,
return_tensors="pt", padding=True)

# Predict label
outputs = model(**inputs)
logits_per_image = outputs.logits_per_image
predicted_label =
labels[logits_per_image.argmax()]

print(f"Predicted Label: {predicted_label}")
```

--> Use CLIP for image retrieval, classification, and AI-powered search engines!

---

2. Converting Speech to Text with Whisper

Whisper is **state-of-the-art for automatic speech recognition (ASR).**

Example: Transcribe Audio with Whisper

python

```python
from transformers import pipeline

# Load ASR pipeline
asr = pipeline("automatic-speech-recognition",
model="openai/whisper-small")

# Transcribe audio file
transcription = asr("sample_audio.mp3")
print(transcription["text"])
```

--> Perfect for chatbots, virtual assistants, and real-time transcription!

Training Custom Transformer Architectures

When pre-trained models **don't meet specific needs**, training a custom transformer from scratch is necessary.

1. Define a Custom Transformer Model

Use **Hugging Face's AutoModel** to modify architectures.

```python
from transformers import AutoModelForSeq2SeqLM,
AutoTokenizer

# Load a transformer model
model =
AutoModelForSeq2SeqLM.from_pretrained("t5-small")
tokenizer = AutoTokenizer.from_pretrained("t5-
small")

# Custom input data
input_text = "Translate English to French: How
are you?"
inputs = tokenizer(input_text,
return_tensors="pt")

# Generate output
output = model.generate(**inputs)
```

```
print(tokenizer.decode(output[0],
skip_special_tokens=True))
```

--> **Modify models for summarization, translation, and specialized NLP tasks!**

Using Hugging Face Reinforcement Learning Models

Hugging Face integrates **Reinforcement Learning (RL)** for AI agents, robotics, and game AI.

1. Install Hugging Face's RL Library

bash

```
pip install transformers[reinforcement-learning]
```

2. Use Stable-Baselines3 for Reinforcement Learning

Train an **AI agent** using the **PPO (Proximal Policy Optimization)** algorithm.

python

```
from stable_baselines3 import PPO
from huggingface_sb3 import load_from_hub

# Load a pre-trained RL model from Hugging Face
Hub
model_id = "sb3/ppo-CartPole-v1"
model = load_from_hub(model_id)
```

```
# Run the trained agent
obs = model.env.reset()
for _ in range(1000):
    action, _states = model.predict(obs)
    obs, rewards, done, info =
model.env.step(action)
    if done:
        break
```

--> **Use RL for game AI, robotics, and automated decision-making!**

Integrating Hugging Face with AutoML for Automated Model Selection

What Is AutoML?

AutoML automates:
--> **Model selection** (choosing the best architecture)
--> **Hyperparameter tuning** (optimizing performance)
--> **Feature engineering** (automated data preprocessing)

---

1. Install AutoML Libraries

```bash

pip install auto-sklearn
```

2. Use AutoML for Automated Model Selection

Example: AutoML for NLP Tasks

```python
from autosklearn.experimental.askl2 import
AutoSklearn2Classifier
from sklearn.feature_extraction.text import
TfidfVectorizer
from sklearn.pipeline import Pipeline
from sklearn.datasets import fetch_20newsgroups

# Load dataset
data = fetch_20newsgroups(subset="train")
vectorizer = TfidfVectorizer()

# Define AutoML pipeline
automl =
AutoSklearn2Classifier(time_left_for_this_task=36
00)

pipeline = Pipeline([
    ("vectorizer", vectorizer),
    ("classifier", automl)
])

# Train AutoML model
pipeline.fit(data.data, data.target)
```

--> **Let AutoML handle model selection and optimization for you!**

Conclusion

This chapter covered **advanced Hugging Face techniques** for AI automation:

--> **Multi-modal transformers for image, text, and audio**
--> **Custom transformer architectures**
--> **Reinforcement learning with Hugging Face RL**
--> **AutoML for automated model selection**

Chapter 9: Best Practices and Troubleshooting

Transformers are powerful, but training and deploying them **can come with challenges**. This chapter covers:

--> **Common issues in transformer training** and how to fix them

--> **Debugging poor model performance**

--> **Ensuring ethical AI and mitigating bias**

--> **Staying up to date with the latest Hugging Face innovations**

By the end of this chapter, you'll know **how to troubleshoot and optimize transformers like a pro**.

Common Issues in Transformer Training

Training transformers **requires massive data, compute, and fine-tuning**. Here are the most common issues:

1. Out-of-Memory (OOM) Errors on GPUs

Transformers are **memory-intensive**. If you get an OOM error, try:

Reduce batch size → Example:

```python

training_args = TrainingArguments(
    per_device_train_batch_size=8,   # Reduce batch size
    gradient_accumulation_steps=4,   # Use accumulation to compensate
```

```
      fp16=True   # Mixed precision training
)
```

Enable gradient checkpointing to reduce memory usage:

```python
python
```

```
model.gradient_checkpointing_enable()
```

Use smaller models like `distilbert` instead of `bert-large-uncased`.

---

2. Slow Training Speed

Use mixed precision training (`fp16`)
Use `torch.compile()` (PyTorch 2.0) for faster execution
Offload computations to multiple GPUs/TPUs

```python
python
```

```
training_args = TrainingArguments(
    per_device_train_batch_size=16,
    dataloader_num_workers=4,   # Increase data
loading speed
    optim="adamw_torch_fused",  # Use fused AdamW
optimizer
)
```

Use Hugging Face's `Accelerate` library for distributed training

```bash
bash

pip install accelerate
python

from accelerate import Accelerator
accelerator = Accelerator()
model, optimizer, train_dataloader =
accelerator.prepare(model, optimizer,
train_dataloader)
```

--> **Faster training = cost-efficient AI models!**

---

3. Poor Model Generalization

If your transformer **memorizes the dataset but performs poorly on new data**, try:

Increase training data → Use **data augmentation** (e.g., back-translation for NLP).
Reduce overfitting → Apply **dropout regularization**:

```python
python

config = AutoConfig.from_pretrained("bert-base-
uncased", hidden_dropout_prob=0.3,
attention_probs_dropout_prob=0.3)
```

Use early stopping to prevent overtraining:

```python
python

early_stopping =
EarlyStoppingCallback(early_stopping_patience=3)
```

```
trainer = Trainer(callbacks=[early_stopping])
```

Debugging Model Performance Problems

When your model **fails to achieve high accuracy**, use these debugging strategies:

1. Check Data Quality

Tokenization Issues?
Ensure text is correctly tokenized:

python

```
tokenizer = AutoTokenizer.from_pretrained("bert-base-uncased")
print(tokenizer.tokenize("Hugging Face is awesome!"))
```

Data Leakage?
Ensure **no overlap between training and test data!**

2. Interpret Model Predictions

Use `transformers.Interpret` for **explainability**
Visualize attention scores → See what the model is focusing on

python

```
from transformers import pipeline
classifier = pipeline("text-classification",
model="bert-base-uncased")
classifier("Hugging Face makes AI easy to use!")
```

Use SHAP or LIME to interpret predictions in production AI.

Ensuring Ethical AI and Bias Mitigation

1. Check for Bias in NLP Models

Transformers **inherit bias from training data**.
Test models on diverse inputs
Use Hugging Face's `bias-mitigation` **tools**

```python
python
```

```
from transformers import BiasMitigationPipeline
bias_pipeline =
BiasMitigationPipeline(model="bert-base-uncased")
bias_pipeline("He is a doctor, she is a nurse.")
```

2. Implement Fairness in AI

Balance datasets → Ensure diverse representation in training data
Apply debiasing techniques → Use **adversarial debiasing**

Enable explainability → AI models must **justify** their predictions

--> **Fair AI = Trustworthy AI!**

Keeping Up with the Latest Hugging Face Updates

Hugging Face **constantly evolves**. Stay updated:

Follow Hugging Face Blog →
https://huggingface.co/blog
Join Hugging Face Discord → Community discussions on AI advances
Use `pip install --upgrade transformers` for the latest features
Check Hugging Face Model Hub → Explore new state-of-the-art models

---

--> **Fix common transformer training issues**
--> **Debug poor model performance efficiently**
--> **Ensure ethical AI and mitigate bias**
--> **Stay up-to-date with Hugging Face innovations**

Conclusion

Hugging Face Transformers have revolutionized **AI automation**, making it easier than ever for professionals to build, deploy, and optimize **state-of-the-art models**.

By mastering Hugging Face's tools and frameworks, you can:

--> **Leverage pre-trained models** for rapid AI development

--> **Fine-tune and optimize** transformers for high performance

--> **Automate AI workflows** with pipelines and model acceleration

--> **Deploy AI models** seamlessly into production environments

Whether you're working in **natural language processing (NLP), computer vision, speech recognition, or multi-modal AI**, Hugging Face **empowers developers** to create **cutting-edge solutions** with minimal effort.

The future of AI automation starts with Hugging Face!

Additional Resources

To continue your journey and stay ahead in AI automation, explore these valuable resources:

Official Documentation & Model Hub

Hugging Face Docs – https://huggingface.co/docs
Transformers Library –
https://huggingface.co/transformers
Hugging Face Model Hub –
https://huggingface.co/models

Research Papers on Transformers

Attention Is All You Need (Vaswani et al.) –
https://arxiv.org/abs/1706.03762
**BERT: Pre-training of Deep Bidirectional
Transformers** – https://arxiv.org/abs/1810.04805
GPT-4 Technical Report –
https://arxiv.org/abs/2303.08774

Online Courses & Tutorials

Hugging Face Course – https://huggingface.co/course
Deep Learning Specialization (Coursera) –
https://www.coursera.org/specializations/deep-learning
Fast.ai NLP Course – https://course.fast.ai

Community Forums & GitHub Repositories

Hugging Face Forums – https://discuss.huggingface.co
GitHub Transformers Repo –
https://github.com/huggingface/transformers
Hugging Face Discord – https://discord.gg/huggingface

What's Next?

Now that you've mastered Hugging Face Transformers, consider:
Building real-world AI applications with your knowledge
Exploring advanced topics like multi-modal transformers and AutoML
Experimenting with cutting-edge models from the Hugging Face Model Hub

AI automation is evolving—stay ahead of the curve!

Table of Contents

www.ingramcontent.com/pod-product-compliance
Lightning Source LLC
LaVergne TN
LVHW051538050326
832903LV00033B/4319